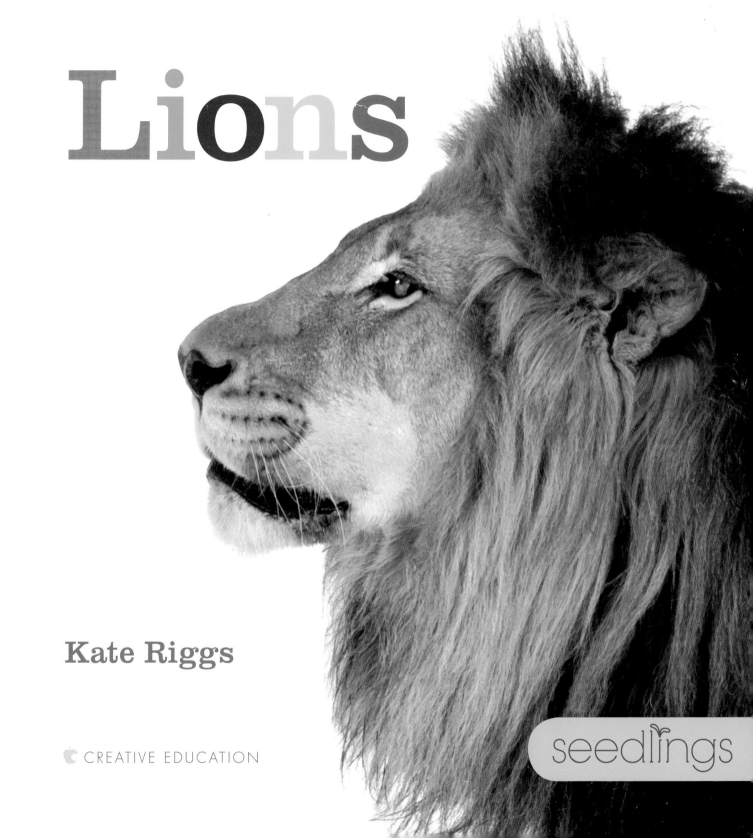

# Lions

Kate Riggs

CREATIVE EDUCATION

seedlings

Published by Creative Education
P.O. Box 227, Mankato, Minnesota 56002
Creative Education is an imprint of
The Creative Company
www.thecreativecompany.us

Design and production by Ellen Huber
Art direction by Rita Marshall
Printed in the United States of America

Photographs by Dreamstime (Cristiaciobanu, Isselee,
Jason Prince), Getty Images (Jonathan and Angela Scott,
Paul Souders), iStockphoto (David T. Gomez, Eric Isselée),
National Geographic Stock (Frans Lanting), Photo
Researchers (Mark Newman/Photo Researchers, Inc.),
Shutterstock (Eric Isselée, Villiers Steyn, Sally Wallis),
Veer (Achim Baqué, space-heater)

Library of Congress Cataloging-in-Publication Data
Riggs, Kate.
Lions / by Kate Riggs.
p. cm. — (Seedlings)
Includes index.
Summary: A kindergarten-level introduction to lions,
covering their growth process, behaviors, the lands they call
home, and such defining physical features as their manes.
ISBN 978-1-60818-277-0
1. Lion—Juvenile literature. I. Title.

QL737.C23R539 2012
599.757—dc23    2011044742

First Edition
9 8 7 6 5 4 3 2 1

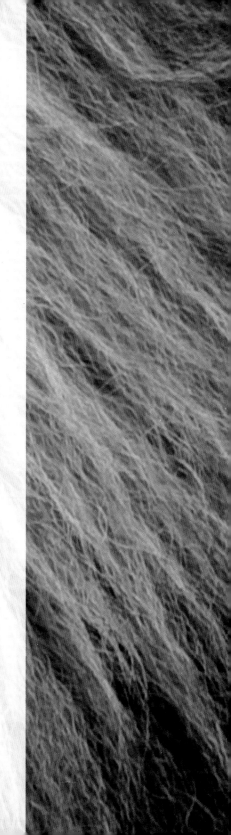

# TABLE OF CONTENTS

Hello, Lions! **5**

Big Cats **7**

Manes and Fur **9**

Claws and Tails **10**

Time to Eat! **12**

Baby Lions **14**

What Do Lions Do? **16**

Goodbye, Lions! **19**

Picture a Lion **20**

Words to Know **22**

Read More **23**

Web Sites **23**

Index **24**

# Hello, lions!

Lions are big cats.
They live in hot parts
of Africa and Asia.

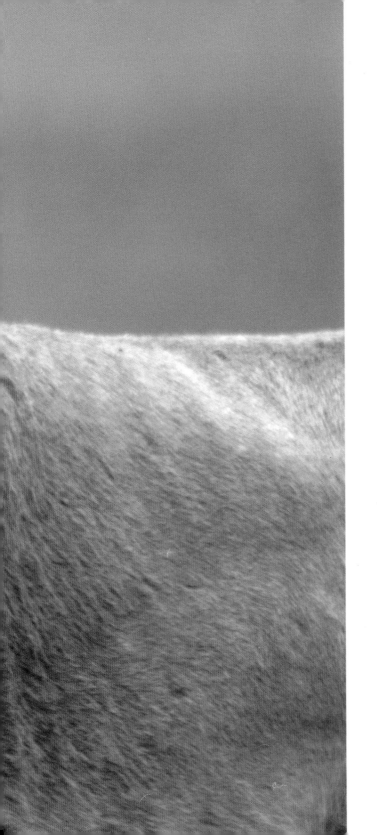

A lion has
yellow or
brown fur.
A male lion
has long
hair on
its neck.
It is called
a mane.

Lions have long tails. They have claws like other big cats.

A lion eats meat.

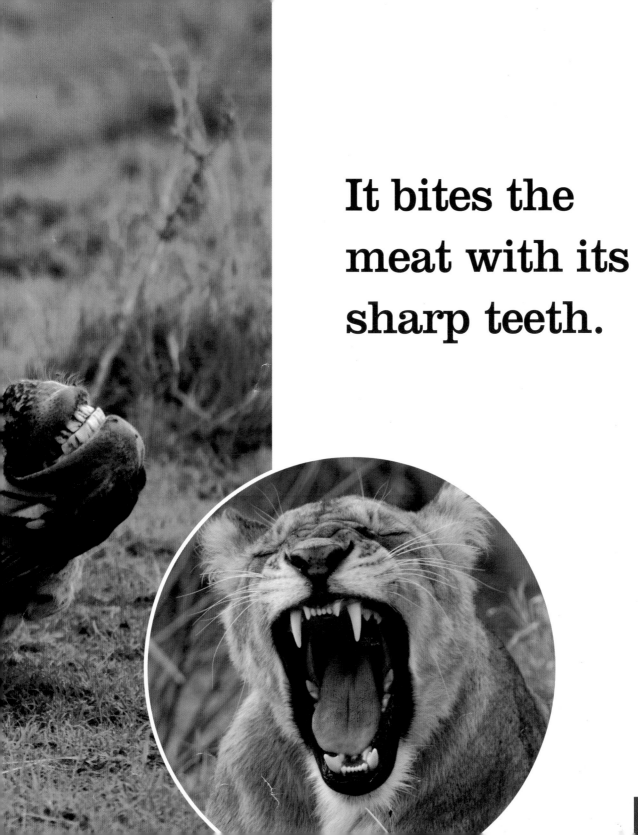

It bites the
meat with its
sharp teeth.

A baby lion is called a cub. A cub lives with other lions in a pride.

Cubs like to play. Then all the lions eat their food.

Lions sleep after they eat.

# Goodbye, lions!

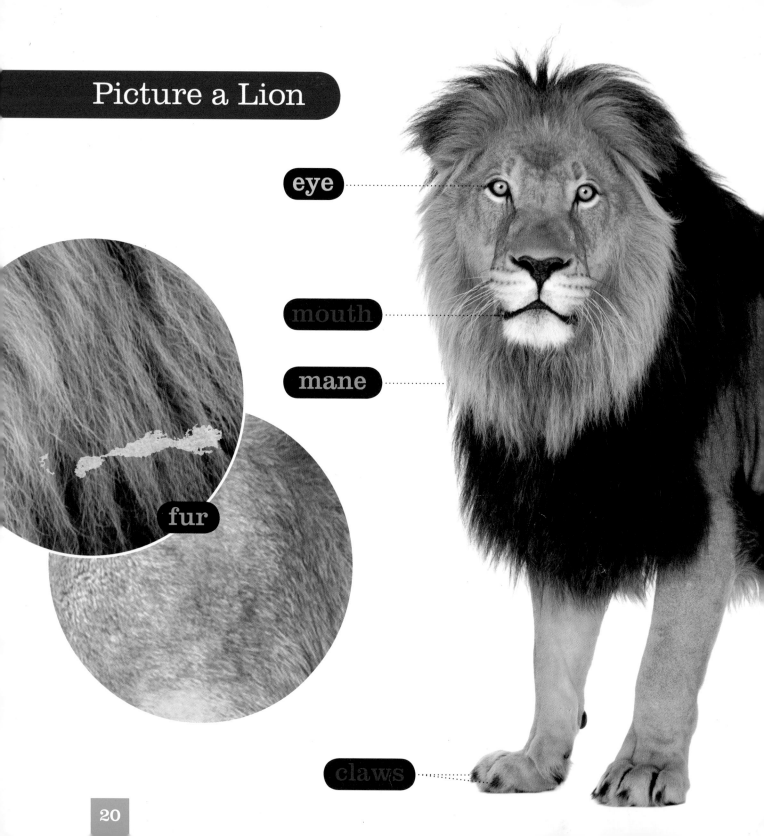

# Picture a Lion

eye

mouth

mane

fur

claws

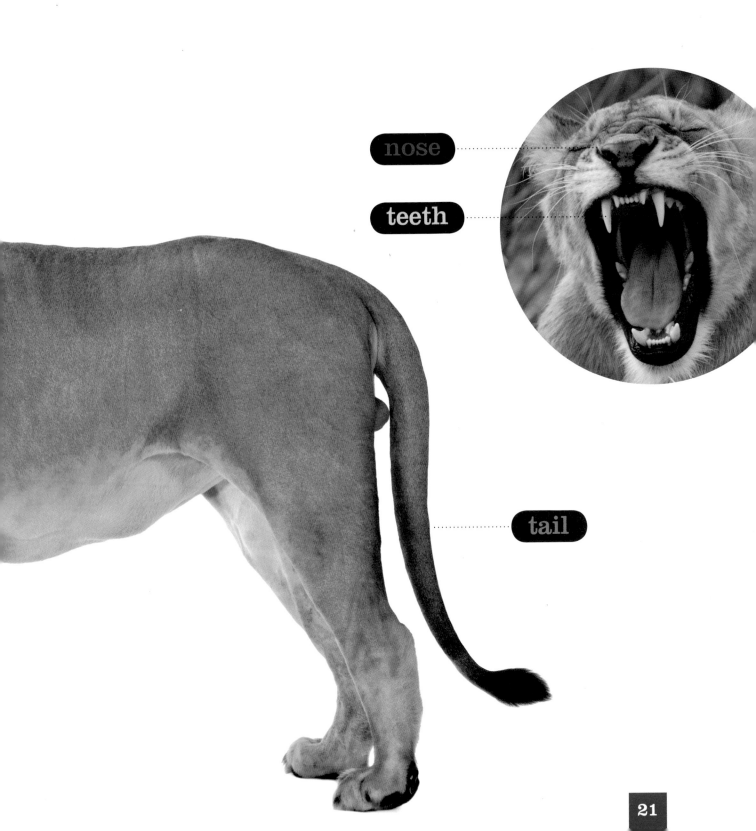

nose

teeth

tail

## Words to Know

**Africa:** the second-biggest piece of land in the world

**Asia:** the biggest piece of land in the world

**fur:** the short hair of an animal

**male:** boy, not girl

**pride:** a group of lions that live together

# Read More

Coxon, Michele. *Look Out, Lion Cub!*
New York: Star Bright Books, 1998.

Shively, Julie. *Baby Lion*.
Nashville: CandyCane Press, 2005.

# Web Sites

DLTK's Jungle Lion Section: Lion Activities
http://www.dltk-kids.com/animals/jungle-lions.html
Choose a craft to do. Have a grown-up help you.

Lion Coloring Pages
http://www.first-school.ws/theme/animals/cp_wild/cp_lion.htm
Click on a lion. Print out the picture to color.

# Index

Africa **7**

Asia **7**

claws **10**

cubs **14, 16**

food **12, 13, 16**

fur **9**

playing **16**

prides **14**

sleeping **17**

tails **10**

teeth **13**